ALMOST ERASED

ALMOST ERASED

Born A. Granger

ReadersMagnet, LLC

ALMOST ERASED
Copyright © 2023 by Born A. Granger

Published in the United States of America

Library of Congress Control Number: 2024903894

ISBN	Paperback:	979-8-89091-406-4
ISBN	Hardback:	979-8-89091-413-2
ISBN	eBook:	979-8-89091-407-1

All rights reserved. No part of this publication may be reproduced, stored in a retrieval system or transmitted in any way by any means, electronic, mechanical, photocopy, recording or otherwise without the prior permission of the author except as provided by USA copyright law.

The opinions expressed by the author are not necessarily those of ReadersMagnet, LLC.

ReadersMagnet, LLC
10620 Treena Street, Suite 230 | San Diego, California, 92131 USA
1.619. 354. 2643 | www.readersmagnet.com

Book design copyright © 2023 by ReadersMagnet, LLC. All rights reserved.

Cover design by Jhie Oraiz
Interior design by Dorothy Lee

I dedicate this book to **Rufus Granger II**, my gentle giant. Daddy, this was tough to relive but necessary to heal. Your only child, Princess.

ALMOST ERASED

I went from being my father's only child, to adopted, married, and divorce. But now delivered from bitterness and unforgiveness. It's not what you call me; it's what I answer to!

Born A. Granger

I also have Bilbo, Dalcour, Fusellier, and Sherwood DNA.

This is the true story of how my only paternal uncle almost succeeded in erasing four generations with one lie.

Exposing the truth hurts even more when it the handprints of your own kinfolks. The truth will set you free and give light to dark places.

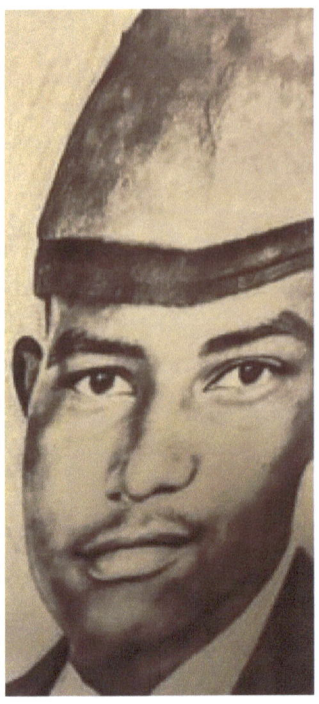

RUFUS GRANGER II
"Lil Bruh"

He stood about 6'4" and was known as a tall drink of water. Every woman wanted, craved, and desired to be on his arm. He was remembered as a big, tall, gentle giant — a handsome, charming, kind-hearted man who would happily give you the shirt off his back. He would help anyone in need, even if that meant borrowing money from his own mother.

My grandmother would say, "Lil Bruh, if they don't pay you back, you still better pay me back!" My Daddy Rufus Granger II is truly missed and will never be forgotten! Daddy was the youngest of two boys. That was how his nickname came to be Lil Bruh.

I could only imagine how my uncle felt, being the first born son and not being named after his father. My Grandparents given my Daddy the honor to carry my Grandfather's name as Rufus Granger II. When it's tradition to name the first born son after the father. I can see how the jealousy and resentment started from birth and this reminds me of Cain and Abel in the Bible.

My daddy with a huge heart never met a stranger. I guess I got that from him — a heart that melts like butter when it comes to caring and helping others in need. I was an only child, born on October 7th in Beaumont, Texas. My father worked as a merchant seaman. He spent a lot of time at sea, away from our family, which quickly resulted in a divorce. Being away four to five months at a time was not easy on a new marriage. I remember traveling from Dallas, Texas, where I was being raised and coming to visit my daddy for the summer, Christmas, Thanksgiving, and Easter vacations in Port Arthur, Texas. Daddy would come and pick me up from my grandmother's houses in Beaumont and Port Arthur, Texas.

Where I would spend most Holidays and Summer breaks with my first cousin. We were close like sisters, and hated when I had to leave. We were only a few months apart but she bossed me around like a big sister showing tough love. My daddy would always remind me I had another cousin. She was the only child of his older brother, who was also like a big sister. Being both of our fathers' only children at that time made us each other's only cousin on that side of the family.

Out of respect to me, my dad didn't allow me to stay over at the house with him and his girlfriend which made me feel left out, as daddy was playing stepdaddy to his girlfriend's two sons. Being older now, I understand the level of protection and respect he had for his Princess!

Growing up, my only cousin and I would share grandmother's bedroom. This was in Port Arthur, Texas. I loved spending time with my dad, grandparents, and my only cousin on his side of the family. I recall hearing my daddy in the next room, getting up for work. At that time, he was working at the Gulf Refinery, along with his father and his older brother. Daddy would knock on grandma's bedroom door as my cousin and I slept in from staying up all night, doing what girl cousins do.

We were always listening to the radio, talking about boys we liked, and discussing which one we would allow to carry our books to class once our break was over. My daddy would say, "Girls I'm leaving for work. Love y'all and mind y'all grandma and papa. I'll see y'all when I get home from work." My cousin and I acted like we were still asleep. Until I realized, "Oh my goodness we need to put our junk food order in before daddy leaves for work." We would spring from bed early in the morning, yelling like roosters. As we raised grandmother's wooden pane window that faced the driveway, I would press the right side of my face against Grandma's window screen, trying not to pop the screen out. I was determined to get a glimpse of my daddy, making sure he heard our junk food order — requesting chips, soda, and candy.

"Daddy, Daddy, you hear me?" I would shout! He would chuckle and respond, "Princess, I thought y'all were asleep!" It didn't matter that I was waking up Grandma's neighbors with my country loudmouth. My daddy didn't care either. As I was his only child and yes, I was spoiled to the bones, Daddy treated me like a little Princess. If I thought I wanted anything, he got it for me. I truly lived up to the name Princess. I also have the same compassion and empathy for others that my dad had for me.

It was near the end of September, and I was looking forward to my 11th birthday. We had family members visiting from

Port Arthur, Texas. I opened the door, excited to see my family visiting from out of town, only to get some shocking news. I was embraced with hugs as my other grandmother shared that she was sorry about what had happened to my Daddy. I was in total shock and disbelief when they had to come clean with the truth and tell me what was going on. My dad had been shot and killed. With no emotion and not clearly understanding, I had so many questions. "When? How? Why?" I asked. I was told on September 28th, a lady shot and killed my daddy. My thoughts were, "Not his longtime girlfriend?" But no, it was a woman at a lounge. I was told my daddy was gone and I would never see him again. Only 10 years old, all I could think was, "This can't be true!" I had just spoken with my daddy, letting him know my birthday was approaching and I was looking forward to seeing him and my cousin for Thanksgiving. He was in his early 30's. Being 10 myself, that seemed old. But not old enough to die.

Daddy, too, would be having a birthday soon in November. I was only 10, thinking 30's was old, but still knowing it was too soon for him to be gone. He was supposed to be here when I turned sweet 16, graduated high school, college, here to walk me down the aisle, see me raise my kids, enjoy his grand and great grandkids. Even today, it's still hard to believe. My daddy is gone!

As I stepped out of the car on 6th St in Port Arthur, Texas, there stood the house I was so familiar with — the fig tree in the backyard, the open mail slot in grandma's front bedroom. All eyes were on me. There were cars parked up and down my grandparents' driveway, the same driveway where I used to yell down my candy order to my daddy. People were speaking French, as this was my grandparents' first language, being from Louisiana. They spoke Creole. I saw people who look like they were white people. Thinking in my head, "I did not know we had white people in our family?" I discovered that I was French Creole on my dad's side and Cherokee Indian on my mom's. That was my blood line but no matter what, I was a proud little black girl. This would explain my long, thick, black hair down my back that was always complimented.

It was my first funeral. I didn't know what to expect. I remember people looking at me and pointing at me repeating, "That's Princess, that's Lil Bruh's daughter." I felt like I was a celebrity. My grandmother had a family member who was a professional opera singer. I remember hearing her music at grandma's house, as everyone was sipping tea. My grandmother was a tall woman which explained my dad's height. My grandfather was an average height Frenchman with grayish blue eyes.

After being shown off to everyone, I was escorted into the house. I remember traveling to Gabriel's Funeral Home for the wake. That's when I learned that a viewing is the place the family would go to see their dead before they go into the ground. I had never seen a dead body but I was determined to touch my daddy for the last time. Everyone at the wake said I look just like my daddy. I stayed focused on the casket which looked like a twin bed on wheels. I had my index finger out and ready. As I took four steps forward towards the bed on wheels, I saw a man who had his eyes closed and that's when it became real. That was my daddy, all stiff and dressed up in a suit. To say "suit casket sharp" was an understatement. Walking a few feet towards him, that's when it all began to hit me. I took five steps back. My family, standing behind me, encouraging me to step forward. I needed that moment to soak up my new reality of living life without my daddy. I took a deep breath as I knew even at the age 10 that it was now or never. If I want to ever touch the man I loved so much — I craved his gentleness as a father — it was my last chance to touch my daddy. In that moment, I took a deep breath, and found the courage to approach the casket. I was not afraid, but I was wondering if my Daddy would rise up. After all, I was only ten and it was my first funeral. I touched my father. It was over! I did it! I touched him for the very last time. He was cold and felt like concrete, Hard like a solid rock.

The next day was October 2nd. It was the day we would lay my father to rest. I was placed into the family car. Wow! My first limousine ride! I did what I saw everyone else do. I heard grandma telling the driver to avoid driving by The Celebrity Lounge where my dad was shot. The location where he died was just a couple of blocks from my grandparents' house. I remember whenever I would visit my grandmother, she would take a weird route home. The image of her son laid shot and killed between a car and the curb, I'm sure stayed in her mind.

It's my understanding that Daddy would frequent The Celebrity Lounge after work for drinks, gambling, and a friendly game of pool with others. Daddy was one of the best pool players in the area. He inherited the trait of gambling from his mother. She would play cards all the time for coins. Once I grew up and became a mother, I would bring my girls to visit my grandparents. Grandmother would give the girls a huge pickle jar of coins to divide among themselves, so that they would have coins to play cards with her. Gambling 101 at an early age was fun memories for my girls with their great grandmother, even if it was only a penny or a nickel a game. Grandmother was true to the games of life and taught me to not take any wooden nickels. She would say things like, "Wooden nickels don't spend" and "Don't let a five-minute thrill turn into a lifetime bill," you know, those old wise tales of wisdom that we don't understand growing up but seem to flow out of our mouths as parents to our own kids. My grandmother had no filter! She said what she wanted when she wanted and how she wanted! She was capable of meeting you on any page. She could be classy and sassy in the same breath.

There I was, a young girl, 10 years old, visiting my grandparents without my daddy. There was a void I couldn't explain. I was a young, outgoing person who never met a stranger, just like my daddy. He could light up any room with his charm and laughter. He was a good man with a big loving heart.

Things shifted with my grandmother; she grew to love me even more, especially since I was her closest connection to my father. She and I became best friends. I could always expect a non-filtered response. I could tell her any and everything without judgment. That's what I loved about her. She would ask me the most personal X-rated questions and wanted details when I was dating. Those who knew her knew how to be ready for anything she would say or ask. She would leave no room for assumption. If she wanted to know, you best believe she would ask you anything with a straight face and always made you laugh with her candid words of expression. Grandmother lost her voice box after choking on piece of food early in her life, but she would express herself with hand gestures to make sure I understood her questions. Grandmother would ask me if I was having sex through hand motions. Wanting to know all my business as we both would laugh. She was my girl and I could ask and tell her anything. To have known her is to have loved her, as I still do! Even after losing her voice and one of her breasts to cancer, Grandmother lived a joyful life. It was never a dull moment with her.

My grandfather died of cancer after working at the Gulf Refinery all his life. They were married over 60 years. Their 50th and 60th wedding anniversaries made the Port Arthur, Texas Newspaper. Granddaddy rode his bike daily to stay healthy and fit. He lived long without his cancer being noticed. Grandmother had no health concerns other than what naturally came with aging. She only took prevention medicine and vitamins. I was able to give her a surprise party in Beaumont, Texas for her 90th birthday. She walked all by herself to the second floor and danced as we celebrated her life. She wore a silk, sea foam green shorts set I had given her as a birthday gift. She trusted me! I said, "Good morning. It's April 3rd, your birthday." Then I gave her the gift and I knew she would put it on.

We drove to a restaurant in Beaumont, Texas to meet other family members from Houston and the surrounding areas of Port Arthur. It's a beautiful memory and now my best friend was gone. Little did I know that would be the last time I would hug and kiss her. French folks kiss on the lips. That was the culture.

I remember when I was married. My husband was confused why I would kiss my grandparents on the lips. But I was raised by Louisiana grandparents; it was normal for me. I could see why a brother from the hood of Sunny South Dallas, Texas, would think that was a little off. But I thought nothing of it. Before she left this earth, my grandmother made sure I knew I was loved. She also wanted me to know that the woman who killed my dad had passed away in a facility. She had kept up with her. This young lady, at the age of 22, had lost her life to the system after killing my father. Texas had the death penalty. So, I'm pretty sure her legal team talked her into pleading insanity versus life in prison. But as my grandmother would say, "If you are not crazy, you will be crazy living in a mental facility."

It's sad how all this unfolded. I'm without a dad. My grandparents are without their son. This 22-year-old woman Charlotte is without her family. Some might not understand why I care. Some people think I should be mad, upset with bitterness and hate. But I am not. Yes, I am sad, upset my daddy is gone and I really miss having him in my life. But I hold onto memories of the car rides from Beaumont to Port Arthur, taking the back roads as my daddy drove his baby blue Buick with the white wall tires. He would take the two lanes back route to feel a sense of living on the edge. When a car in front of him was going too slow, Daddy would pull over to the opposite traffic lane and pass the car with just enough time to pull back into his lane to avoid oncoming traffic.

As a kid, I wasn't thinking that was dangerous. I just knew in Daddy's Care, I was safe no matter what! I did get butterflies riding in the car with my dad. It was scary and fun at the same time. I would ask him to do it again. He would respond by speeding up to a car and passing again. Grandmother would say, "God takes care of babies and fools."

But I was having fun. It was the same feeling I would get riding my bike down Boulder Street in Oak Cliff, Texas. It was like an amusement park ride. Now, life without him now is rough.

I remember when both of my grandparents were living. Grandmother would wake up in the middle of the night with a cramp in her leg. She would have one hand holding the cramping leg and her other hand holding her voice box to speak. I understood by her movements that she was in pain. I would reach to help her, but grandmother would quickly decline my gesture to help. She would communicate that her leg cramp was near her upper leg area. I would yell for grandpa who was sleeping down the hall in the next bedroom. Grandfather would come into the bedroom with a banana already peeled. He knew just what the doctor ordered to get rid of grandmother's leg cramp. As he was familiar and experienced in taking care of her nightly leg cramps, I felt out of place. She needed him to rub her leg. But with me in the room, he felt uncomfortable. So, Grandpa handed the banana to her and left the room. Grandmother and I must have laughed about that all night. As she walked around the bedroom placing pressure on her leg while eating her banana, we were laughing uncontrollably. It happened so fast. I didn't know what to do. Grandmother's breathing sounded off without her voice box so I panicked. But afterwards, we laughed and shared stories about my dad into the night, until we talked ourselves back to sleep.

Another fond memory I have was when Grandmother was up early in the morning, fixing breakfasts with fig preserve. She had a fig tree in the back yard, so my grandparents had figs preserved in mason jars everywhere. I didn't like figs but I would enjoy going to Dorothy's Back Porch, or was it Dorothy's Front Porch Restaurant? My memory escapes me. Anyway, grandmother would order frog legs and I was always excited to get the change after grandmother paid the bill. We would buy fish food and feed the fish in the pond at the restaurant. That was the best part for me! I went solely for the excitement of feeding the fish and watching grandmother eat frog legs. She said it tasted like chicken but I could never get over the fact that it was a frog! So, I would stare in awe as grandmother sucked the meat off a frog's leg as if it were a chicken bone.

Grandmother and I would visit my dad's gravesite and I would get mad at any ant piles near my dad's grave. I needed something to blame, thinking that only if my dad was not always away at sea, his marriage could have worked out and maybe my Daddy would still be alive.

Grandma would take me to see my cousin and we all would have brunch at Pick a Dilly's restaurant and then come home and eat homemade link sausages with Grandpa for dinner. My cousin and I would pop popcorn after our grandparents went to sleep. Grandpa would wake up the next morning and realize my cousin and I had poured the leftover popcorn kernels down the kitchen drain. Grandpa was mad as hell. I knew he was mad when he would start cursing in French, looking just like a black Archie Bunker. But he loved to dance and had a personality like George Jefferson. I miss them.

It was never a dull moment when I would come and visit. I remember it like it was yesterday, coming face to face with a live bull at my great-grandmother's house after Dad's death. Grandmother would take my cousin and I to visit her mother in Louisiana. She was known as Mrs. Archie, after her first late husband Mr. Archie Dalcour.

Great-grandmother was highly respected, even by white people, in her day. I hear stories of her trading eggs or goose livestock for her favorite Mogen David wine. But my greatest memory of her is when she stood between me and the bull as my protector. She waved a broom in one hand and with her other hand, waved at my cousin and I to get onto her porch. She shouted for me to take off the red britches I was wearing!

You should have seen my cousin and I, trying to pull off my red britches over my cowboy boots. I didn't know a bull would charge after anything that was red. I came to the swamps of Louisiana in my red pants, cowboy hat, and boots. With the big Texas belt buckle, I was too cute. But I would soon find myself on the porch in my underwear and boots. My great grandmother saved my life that day. I am forever grateful and gain a new level of respect for the old lady whom I had only met a few times in my life.

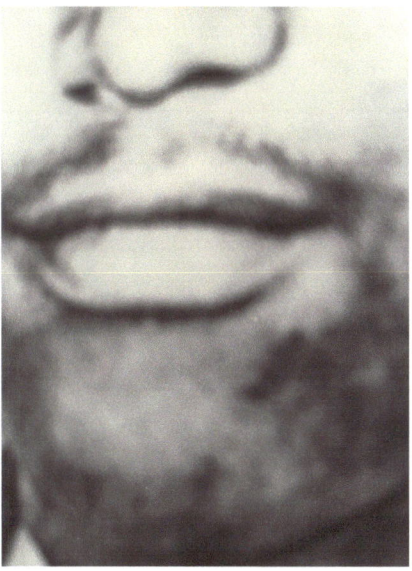

Now Daddy's gone and my grandparents are all gone. The closest connection to my dad is my uncle and cousin on my father's side. I felt emotionally isolated with no true connection with the rest of the family. I wasn't sure if I wanted to attend the family reunion. It wasn't until my oldest daughter researched Charlottes family and found them on facebook. The healing of forgiveness began. I spoke to Charlotte's brother: we had no bitter feelings towards one other. I wanted to know if Ms. Charlotte had kids. My daddy's ex-girlfriend said Charlotte was a woman of the streets but after speaking to Charlotte's brother, I learned my daddy gave Ms. Charlotte a gun to protect herself. Charlotte would work late hours at The Celebrity Lounge where Daddy frequently visited. It was a place where people went to drink and play pool. Folks liked to gamble against daddy, him being one of the best pool sharks in Port Arthur, Texas. That gun was given as a means of protection, but I often wonder if that's the same gun that she used to kill my daddy?

Prior to my father's tragic death, he had been in a steady, long-term relationship with an older woman after his divorce. I was told Daddy was being nice to Charlotte. My daddy was a good-looking brother with money, and many women were attracted to him. It was my understanding that that morning, Charlotte and my daddy got into an argument, perhaps fueled by jealousy of other women and/or her romantic feelings for my father. That argument led to his death. It's become apparent to me, as an adult now. I've been searching and looking for a father in my own relationship.

There's so many childhood memories flooding my mind as I contemplated attending my family reunion — memories of visiting my grandparents after dad's funeral, memories of my grandmother, parading me around like a Princess, my great-grandmother saving me from the charging bull, remembering that last touch of my father's cold forehead and seeing him for the very last time. I never knew how much I would miss him until now.

I'm all grown up and now a grandmother myself, but I still miss my daddy! Today, I still have those special memories and I keep them tucked away in my heart. I miss my Daddy so much!! He's not here in the physical but I now know The Father to the fatherless.

Now understanding through my own divorce I have accepted Jesus Christ as my Lord and Savior. I can now trace back over my 50 plus years and see my steps order in His Word with a hedge of protection over my life, my daughters' and grandkids' even with the relocation from Dallas, TX to Jacksonville, FL, where I have resided for 14 years now.

My girls didn't really know my Dad's family. Whenever my first grandson heard us talk about how much he favored his grandfather, he always had questions about him and what happened. When my oldest daughter found Charlotte's brother, forgiveness took place. What the devil meant for evil, God got the glory! I have no hatred nor bitterness towards Charlotte nor her family. Like my father, I'm a forgiving person.

After exploring information and family research, I learned there were legal documents signed by my uncle identifying "one" child was born to my grandparents. This false documentation of the word "ONE" resulted in financial gain that excluded me from my dad's inheritance. I repeatedly called my uncle to get an understanding, but he never returned any of my phone calls. I called my only cousin, his daughter, to discuss the deceptive document of proof that hopefully wouldn't put a wedge on our relationship. Unfortunately, she wasn't very surprised. I didn't know how to process the selfish acts of my uncle. It felt like my father was being murdered all over again. My father being excluded from family history was upsetting. Inheritance that was stolen from his legacy was upsetting. However, the most hurtful were the generations of lives that could have been erased with one lie, the lie that states my grandparents Rufus and Maudry Granger had "ONE" child. My uncle owes the truth to my daughters, my five grandchildren, and myself. Four generations were directly and indirectly negatively impacted the family history because of greed.

I'm in the process of getting the court documents reversed. I have forgiven my uncle; however, I do want him to know how hurtful his actions were to me and our family. I pray that my uncle repents of his sins and asks for Abba Father for forgiveness. Forgive himself, as I forgive, for my own self-healing. In the act of denying ALMOST ERASED 4 generations but never will I deny who I am. I am a Dalcour, born a Granger.

I was not sure if I wanted to share and expose the truth, but like my grandmother would say, "The truth hurts, but the truth will set you free." It's like medicine; open up and swallow. It doesn't taste good but it's good for you! The only question I have for my only uncle, my dad's big brother is, "Was it worth it?" My family and I may have been mishandled, but never will be erased! What was done in the dark has come to the light!

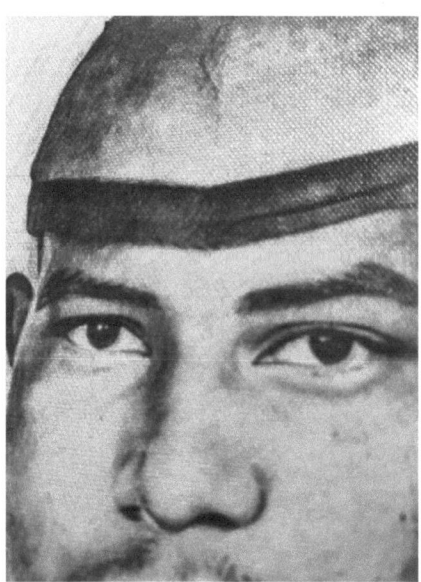

Memories dance in my head as I prepare to attend my Dalcour Family Reunion. Dalcour was my grandmother's maiden name. I may come face to face with the man who disowned his own brother, in an act of greed that threatened the entire Dalcour and Granger family history. But I will show him the love of Christ! If I can forgive Charlotte, the woman who took my Daddy's life, I forgive my Daddy's brother, my uncle who denies his own 'Lil Bruh'. When you deny your own brother. You deny me, your only niece Princess.

(Ephesians 4:31-32) Don't Be Bitter; Forgiveness is Better

I'm too a Granger! It's not what you call me. It's what I answered to!

"Daddy, you are missed and never forgotten!"

"Daddy, let me introduce you to your family."

"Often Imitated but Never Duplicated and Never Erased!"

www.ingramcontent.com/pod-product-compliance
Lightning Source LLC
LaVergne TN
LVHW070048070526
838201LV00036B/360